BERKSHIRE TRACTION

Simon Lindsell

AMBERLEY

Front Cover: 60099 is seen at Thatcham on 20 December 2013 with the late-running 6A11 Robeston Refinery loaded oil train to Theale. 60099 originally carried the name *Ben More Assynt*, which is the name of a Scottish mountain.

Rear Cover: HST set 253 018 at Basildon on 12 June 1978. The leading power car is 43037, which was retired from service with Great Western Railway in 2019. (John Dedman)

First published 2019

Amberley Publishing
The Hill, Stroud
Gloucestershire, GL5 4EP

www.amberley-books.com

Copyright © Simon Lindsell, 2019

The right of Simon Lindsell to be identified as the Author of this work has been asserted in accordance with the Copyrights, Designs and Patents Act 1988.

ISBN 978 1 4456 9477 1 (print)
ISBN 978 1 4456 9478 8 (ebook)

British Library Cataloguing in Publication Data. A catalogue record for this book is available from the British Library.

Origination by Amberley Publishing.
Printed in the UK.

Introduction

Like so many travellers, our journey begins at Reading, which is the centre of railway operations in Berkshire. From Reading we will travel to the extremities of Berkshire, along the Great Western main line to Langley in the east and Lower Basildon in the west, along the Berks and Hants route as far as Hungerford and south of the line to Basingstoke as far as Mortimer. Also covered are the former southern routes to London via Ascot and to Redhill as far as Sandhurst. Photographs are arranged in rough geographical order radiating from Reading along each line.

The main station at Reading has been redeveloped twice during our period of study. In 1989 a brand new station concourse was opened by InterCity, which included the Brunel shopping arcade, opened on the western end of the old Reading Southern station site, linked to the platforms of the main station by a new footbridge. At the same time a new multilevel station car park was built on the site of the former goods yard and signal works to the north of the station, and linked to the same footbridge. The 1860s station building was converted into The Three Guineas pub. The Queen reopened the station on 4 April 1989.

By 2007 the station had become an acknowledged bottleneck on the railway network, with passenger trains often needing to wait outside the station for a platform to become available. This was caused by the limited number of through platforms, the flat junctions immediately east and west of the station and the need for cross-country services to and from Bournemouth to reverse direction in the station. The Great Western main line at Reading has two pairs of tracks: the main lines on the southern side and the relief lines on the northern side. Trains transferring between the relief lines and the lines that run through Reading West (to Taunton and Basingstoke) had to cross the main lines. Those trains – especially slow-moving freight trains – blocked the paths of trains on the main lines.

On 10 September 2008 Network Rail unveiled a £400 million regeneration and reconfiguration of Reading station and surrounding track layout. The following changes were made:

The addition of five new platforms; four new through platforms on the northern side and an extra bay platform for the former southern lines.

A new footbridge on the western side of the station, replacing the 1989 footbridge; this also included a new entrance on the southern side, for ticket holders only.

A new street-level entrance and ticket office on the northern side of the station.

The original subway was converted into a pedestrian underpass between the two sides of the station, with no access to the platforms.

Cow Lane Bridge under the tracks was made two-way with a cycle path.

A flyover to the west of the station to allow fast trains on the main lines to cross over the lines to Reading West, replacing the flat junction.

A track beneath the flyover to provide a connection between Reading West and the relief lines.

The train care depot was moved from within the triangle of lines which provided links to the east and west from Reading West station to the north side of the main line on the site of Reading West Junction sidings.

Overhead electrification to link in with the Great Western main line electrification, which was completed in time for electric trains to commence service between Paddington and Didcot Parkway on 2 January 2018.

The improvements have allowed capacity for at least four extra trains in each direction every hour and six extra freight trains a day.

Passenger journeys through Berkshire were revolutionised in the mid-1970s with the introduction of the InterCity High Speed Train (HST).

A team of engineers were assembled at the Railway Technical Centre in Derby in the early 1960s with the aim of designing and developing an Advanced Passenger Train (APT) that would be capable of at least 125 mph and incorporate many features not previously seen on British railways – such as tilting to allow higher speeds on curves.

The APT project had suffered repeated delays and in 1970 the British Railways Board (BRB) decided that it was not sufficiently developed to modernise the railways in the short term. Therefore the BRB authorised the development of a high-speed diesel train for short-term use until the APT was able to take over. Thus the HST was born.

On 4 October 1976 a partial service of HSTs running at 125 mph began on the Western Region. A radical update of the standard BR livery on the power cars was complemented by the InterCity 125 branding, which also appeared on timetables and promotional literature. By the start of the summer timetable in May 1977, the full complement of twenty-seven Class 253 sets (253001–253027) was in service on the Western Region, completely replacing locomotive-hauled trains on the Bristol and South Wales routes. Passenger volumes on the trains rapidly increased due to the speed and frequency of the service – an effect previously seen only when electric trains had replaced diesel or steam services. The displacement by HSTs of the Class 50 locomotives to slower services effectively finished off the last Class 52 diesel-hydraulics by early 1977.

From introduction, maintenance has always been provided from Old Oak Common and St Philip's Marsh, with Laira also carrying out maintenance once services to Devon and Cornwall were introduced in 1979.

The Class 47 locomotives still operated the cross-country services from Cornwall and South Wales to the North East via the Cross Country route, as well as London to the Midlands/Welsh Marches. However, Class 43s also replaced these services once the third batch of power cars was delivered. All these HSTs consisted of a 2+7 formation, normally with two first-class coaches, a buffet car, and four second-class coaches, all sandwiched between two power cars. They were later expanded to a 2+8 formation, adding an extra second-class coach.

Great Western Railway was formed out of the privatisation of British Rail and operated the InterCity routes from London Paddington to the west of England. In 1998 FirstGroup acquired Great Western Railway and rebranded it First Great Western. InterCity 125s continued to work the same diagrams they had under British Rail, albeit in a different livery.

Great Western Railway used its large fleet of forty-three HST sets to operate most intercity services from Paddington, as well as some commuter services to Westbury, Taunton and Exeter St Davids. As of 2012 all First Great Western's intercity services were worked by InterCity 125 sets with the exception of sleeper services and certain Cotswold line services. This lasted until 2019, when the introduction of the Class 800s resulted in the HSTs being either taken off lease or refurbished with power doors and retention toilets to form four coach sets for use on services in the West Country and Wales.

Revolution returned to the railways of Berkshire around forty years later with overhead electrification, which made possible the entry into service of the Class 800 Intercity Express Train (IET). As part of the UK Government's Intercity Express Programme (IEP), the Class 800 units are replacements for the HSTs, which currently operate services on the Great Western main line. Great Western Railway will operate three variants of Class 800.

The Class 800s are being assembled at the Hitachi Newton Aycliffe facility from bodyshells shipped from the Kasado plant in Japan; no body construction takes place in the UK. The Great Western Railway fleet comprises classes 800, 800/3 and 802 and started entering service in October 2017.

The Class 800s are bimodal multiple units able to draw power from electrified overhead lines where available or underfloor diesel engines when outside the electrified network. The train specification requires that this changeover can occur at line speed. The Class 800 and the Class 802 electro-diesel or bimodal units have three diesel engines per five car set and five diesel engines per nine car set.

The Class 800/3 units were originally classified as pure electric Class 801 units but due to delays in the GWML electrification they were built with larger than originally specified fuel tanks so they can run in regular service using their diesel engines.

The Class 802 is similar to the Class 800 but has uprated diesel engines and larger fuel tanks for working beyond the scope of the GWML electrification over the steep South Devon banks. Unlike the Class 800s, the Class 802 are built at Hitachi's Pistoia Works in Italy and brought to the UK through the Channel Tunnel.

Freight services through Berkshire have also seen a dramatic change in the last forty years with the change from traditional vacuum braked short wheelbase wagons to air braked high capacity bogie wagons with a gross laden weight of 100 tons each. Train lengths have also increased with the introduction of the Class 59s for mendip stone traffic and the Class 66s for most other freight services.

During the early 1980s Foster Yeoman were suffering with the poor reliability of the motive power provided by British Rail for their stone trains. After much investigation they decided to buy their own locomotives and, having had a positive experience with an American general motors SW1001 switcher at Merehead, turned to GM to produce what became the Class 59. The Class 59 is basically an SD40-2 scaled down to fit within the UK loading gauge. 59001 to 59004 were delivered in January 1986 and entered traffic in February 1986. A fifth Class 59, 59005, was delivered in June 1989.

Having witnessed the success of the Foster Yeoman Class 59s, ARC bought four Class 59s numbered 59101 to 59104, which entered service in 1990.

National Power purchased six Class 59s, numbered 59201 to 59206 and based at a purpose-built depot adjacent to Ferrybridge power station, to work trains for the Aire Valley power stations. In the late 1990s the entire National Power rail operation was sold to EWS and the 59/2s moved to Westbury for use on trains from the Mendip stone quarries.

The introduction of the Class 59s enabled the running of jumbo stone trains of as many as forty-two wagons, which combine the trains or 'portions' for up to three of the south-eastern stone terminals. The 'portions' are split and remarshalled at Acton Yard and worked separately to and from their destinations.

On the privatisation of British Rail's freight operations in 1996, a number of the newly privatised rail freight companies – Transrail, Mainline, Loadhaul, and later Railfreight Distribution and Rail Express Systems – were bought by Wisconsin Central Transportation and combined to become English Welsh & Scottish Railways (EWS).

EWS inherited a fleet of 1,600 mainly diesel locomotives, with an average age of over thirty years. To enable it to offer its stated lower pricing to customers, EWS needed to reduce operating costs and raise availability.

After reviewing the existing Class 59, EWS approached its builder Electro-Motive Diesel (EMD), then a division of General Motors. EMD offered their JT42CWR model, which had the same loading gauge-passing bodyshell as the Class 59. The engine and traction motors were different models to enable higher speeds, and the Class 66s incorporated General Motors' version of a 'self-steering bogie', known as a 'radial truck' in America, was designed to reduce track wear and increase adhesion on curves.

EWS placed an order for 250 Class 66s in May 1996 to be built at the EMD plant in London, Ontario, Canada. Financed by Locomotion Capital (later Angel Trains), the first locomotives were ready in early 1998 – the fastest delivery of an all-new locomotive type by GM.

Once the Class 66s began entering service in significant numbers that spelt the end for the majority of existing British-built diesel classes. Only the Class 60s survive in EWS/DB regular service today, although other classes are still used by other operators.

Once the success of the EWS Class 66 fleet was noted, other operators quickly followed suit and today Class 66s from EWS/DB, Freightliner, GBRF and to a lesser extent Colas Rail Freight are regularly seen hauling freight through Berkshire. The Direct Rail Services (DRS) Class 66s shown in this book are actually in use by Freightliner as 66411 to 66420 were returned to the leasing company by DRS and subsequently leased out to Freightliner.

So how did I come to be sitting here writing this book? It was my dad who got me interested in railways and over the years railway photography has grown into something of an obsession. It started local to my home town of Andover but now I travel all over the UK in pursuit of interesting trains and locations. It was the encouragement of other photographers who I met on my travels that led me to set up my Flickr site (https://www.flickr.com/photos/offroadanonymous/). As my photos are now available to a wider audience I strive to achieve better results, seek out different locations and try new things. I was contacted by Amberley Publishing who liked what they saw on Flickr and asked if I would be prepared to write a book on the railways of Berkshire. I agreed and here we are.

My thanks go out to all those photographers who have generously allowed their work to be included in this book. Special thanks go out to John Dedman and Simon Howard, whose photographs have proved invaluable in expanding the scope of this book.

All photos are by the author unless credited.

33104 has just taken over an Inter-Regional service at Reading, heading to Bournemouth, on 13 July 1976. 47078 *Sir Daniel Gooch* is waiting on the centre road for its next duty. (John Dedman)

Class 52 D1048 *Western Lady* is approaching Reading station from the London direction with a train load of empty MSV stone wagons on 13 July 1976. This was one of the last Western Class 52 diesels I photographed and was probably heading for Westbury and one of the Somerset stone quarries. (John Dedman)

In original BR blue livery 50008 is arriving at Reading on 13 July 1976 with a set of mark two air-conditioned coaches. There is no buffet car, which is unusual for this type of formation. 50008 was named in September 1978 after the dreadnought HMS *Thunderer*, which was built in 1911. (John Dedman)

50027 is speeding through Reading with an Up test train on 13 July 1976. This loco was named *Lion* in April 1978 after the battlecruiser HMS *Lion*, which was built in 1909. This particular test train was used from September 1971 as a test bed to prove the Advanced Passenger Train – experimental suspension, tilting and braking systems. Its two central cars (PC3 – RDB975634 and PC4 – RDB975635) each have one mock-up power bogie (P) and are connected with an unpowered articulated trailer bogie (0) in between, hence the nickname 'P-O-P'. (John Dedman)

Class 205 diesel electric three-car multiple unit 1111 is seen arriving at Reading on 2 July 1977. The head-code 88 shows it has come from the Tonbridge route. (John Dedman)

A greatly missed sight, this parcels train of mainly blue and track grime-coloured GUVs is hauled by a 'skinhead' Class 31, in this case 31144. Long before the catenary masts were to appear and ruin the scene. Taken on a grey overcast 8 May 1985. (Pete Nurse)

A contrast of cab front design, 31250 has the Domino marker lights in its head-code box. Its long train of ballast wagons squeal and rattle over the crossovers heading west on 8 May 1985. (Pete Nurse)

97650 was built by Ruston and Hornsby in 1953 and was used by the Western Region Civil Engineer's department at Reading. It was originally numbered PWM650 and was renumbered into the 97 series around 1980. It is seen here in 1985 at a signal check in the station hauling a crane. This loco has been preserved and is at the Lincolnshire Wolds Railway. (John Fox)

56045 heading east and about to pass through Reading passenger platforms with a long rake of Yeoman Hoppers from Merehead Quarry, perhaps en route to Acton Yard on 8 May 1985. It was the unreliability of these handsome locomotives that brought about the introduction of the General Motors Class 59 of course and look where that led! After being withdrawn in 1999, 56045 was sold to Fastline Ltd, a subsidiary of the railway maintenance contractor Jarvis, overhauled and renumbered as 56301. After the collapse of Fastline, 56301 was sold in preservation and is now owned by the Class 56 Group. (Pete Nurse)

Changing tracks at Reading with empty 100-ton tank wagons on 6C08, the 13.30 Langley to Robeston Sidings is a work-worn 56053 that sounds superb. A well-filled gas holder watches over the spectacle on 8 May 1985! Reading was a wonderful place back then with a good selection of trains passing to capture our attention. (Pete Nurse)

47705 approaches Reading on 4 August 1990 with a passenger service from Oxford to London Paddington. The train makes for an impressive sight with the loco and all the coaches in matching Network SouthEast livery. (Simon Howard)

Railfreight red stripe liveried 37371 is partnered by Railfreight Petroleum liveried 37220 *Westerleigh* as they approach Reading station with 6A08, the 00:40 Waterstone Refinery to Langley oil terminal, 21 May 1992. (John Dedman)

On 21 May 1992 47431, in large logo livery, is slowing for the Reading stop at 07:08 with an Up early morning commuter service to Paddington composed of Network SouthEast mark two coaches. 47431 had a painted name of *Silurian*, which it only carried for two years. (John Dedman)

InterCity liveried 47832 *Tamar* is arriving at Reading with an Up InterCity service on 21 May 1992. Like so many Class 47s, 47832 has carried a number of liveries since this photograph was taken including First Great Western green, FM Rail, Victa Westlink Rail, Stobart, DRS Compass, Northern Belle Pullman and, at the time of writing, West Coast Railway Company maroon. (John Dedman)

43031 trails a westbound passenger service heading away from Reading station on 5 May 2003. Berkshire would soon miss the scream of the Paxman Valenta 12RP200L engine as the Great Western fleet of HSTs were re-engined with MTU 16V4000 R41R engines from 2005. (Simon Howard)

67019 stands at Reading station on 12 April 2001 with the 1M06 Swansea to Willesden Railnet Terminal mail train. 67029 was on the other end of the train.

47811 arrives at Reading station platform 4 with a rake of First Great Western mark two coaches on 10 August 2001, working a service from London Paddington to the west of England. After First Great Western abandoned loco-hauled services, 47811 was sold to Freightliner, who last used it as a super shunter at Crewe Basford Hall Yard.

47831 arrives at Reading station platform 9 on 10 August 2001 with a Virgin Cross Country service. 47831 carried the name *Bolton Wanderer* from June 1989 until September 2002. After withdrawal, 47831 entered the Class 57 rebuilding program, donating parts for the creation of the Virgin Trains Class 57/3 numbered 57310. Sixteen Class 57/3 were built by Brush Traction for use by Virgin Trains as rescue locomotives or thunderbirds on the West Coast Main Line. The first, 57301, emerged from Brush Traction in June 2002.

57601 is entering Reading station on 10 August 2001 with the 09:20 Plymouth to London Paddington. This was the first Class 57 with electric train heat capability, and was unveiled at Brush Traction's Loughborough works on 24 March 2001 having been built using parts from 47165, 47590 and 47825. Its distinctive purple and silver livery earned it the nickname Purple Ronnie and it spent several months on test with First Great Western. In April 2003 it was sold to the West Coast Railway Company and remains in service with them to this day.

56129 is entering Reading station on 14 September 2002 with Pathfinder Tours 'The Soton Vinegar' charter train from Derby to Southampton, which the Class 56 worked from Gloucester to Willesden South West Sidings. 56129 was withdrawn in July 2003 at Thornaby depot and scrapped at EMR Hartlepool.

37427 and 37669 stand on the goods lines at Reading station on 5 February 2005 with Pathfinder Tours 'The East-Ender' Crewe to London Liverpool Street (1Z73). The 37s were swapped for 73204 and 73205 here at Reading. At this time, 37427 carried the unofficial name *Bont y Brymo*.

After the loco swap, 73204 and 73205 await departure from Reading on 5 February 2005 with Pathfinder Tours 'The East-Ender' Crewe to London Liverpool Street (1Z73). All the GBRF Class 73s carry the names of female staff members; 73204 is named *Janice* and 73205 is named *Jeanette*.

HST power car 43017 is heading an Up HST service as it slows for the Reading stop on 13 September 2006. 43017 has carried the names *HTV West* and *Hannahs* - discoverhannahs.org. (John Dedman)

57602 *Restormel Castle* stands in Reading station platform 4 on 3 January 2011 with the 1C99 London Paddington to Penzance Down sleeper service. Following the trial with 57601, First Great Western placed an order for four Class 57/6 to work the Night Riviera sleeper service between London Paddington and Penzance. 57602 was rebuilt from 47337 and introduced into service in November 2003. (Simon Howard)

55009 *Alycidon* smokes out the whole of Reading station while working 1Z56 'Golden Jubilee Pullman' from Kidderminster to London Victoria on 16 May 2015. (Simon Howard)

DRS loco 37424/558 *Avro Vulcan XH558* stands in Reading station on 15 March 2017 while working 2Z02 Reading to Acton with the observation saloon *Caroline*. This Class 37 was named *Avro Vulcan XH558* at the Crewe Gresty Bridge open day in 2016. Observation saloon *Caroline* is a former Hastings unit restaurant coach. (Simon Howard)

During 2018 HST sets were getting scarcer as the year went by as they were being replaced by the new Class 800 Intercity Express Train units. Here the new order is represented by 800304, which waits to depart Reading for Paddington on 27 June 2018. (John Dedman)

57009 Freightliner *Venturer* is passing Reading West station on 10 August 2001 with the 4O24 Crewe Basford Hall Yard to Southampton Maritime Container Terminal container train. In the early years of privatisation Freightliner was desperately short of reliable motive power. They teamed up with Porterbrook Leasing and Brush Traction to produce a fleet of twelve Class 57s, rebuilding Class 47s with refurbished General Motors 645-12E3 engines supplied by VMV Enterprises in the USA and Brush BA1101A alternators as fitted to the Class 56. 57009 was rebuilt from 47079 and introduced into service in December 1999. When Freightliner ceased to operate its Class 57s in favour of Class 66s, 57009 was one of nine Class 57s that were taken over by Direct Rail Services.

59002 *Alan J Day* is passing Reading West station on 19 June 2001 with the 7V67 Sevington Sidings to Merehead quarry empty stone train. 59002 was originally named *Yeoman Enterprise* but was renamed *Alan J Day* at Cranmore on the East Somerset Railway on 21 June 1996 after one of the Foster Yeoman managing directors. 59002 was the only Class 59 painted in the short-lived Mendip Rail green and orange livery, which resulted from the merger of the Foster Yeoman and Hanson rail operations, forming Mendip Rail.

58037 *Worksop Depot* is passing Reading West station on 19 June 2001 with the 7026 Didcot Yard to Eastleigh East Yard engineers train. 58037 was withdrawn in April 2002 at Eastleigh depot and has since been scrapped.

58031 is passing Reading West station on 19 June 2001 with the lightly loaded 6S65 Eastleigh East Yard to Mossend enterprise train. After withdrawal from regular EWS service, 58031 was sent to Spain to work for Continental Rail on construction of the AVE high speed network.

60009 is passing Reading West station on 22 December 2006 with the 6E10 Theale to Lindsey Refinery empty oil train. At this time the oil terminal at Theale was receiving trains from both Robeston refinery in West Wales and Lindsey refinery on Humberside, averaging six trains a week. 60009 was originally named *Carnedd Dafydd*, which is the name of a Welsh mountain.

37884 passes through Sonning cutting on 20 December 2017 with the 5Q74 Bletchley to Reading depot delivering 387173 to Reading depot ready to enter service with First Great Western. 37884 has previously carried the name *Gartcosh*.

57603 *Tintagel Castle* passes through Sonning cutting on 21 December 2017 with the heavily delayed 5A40 Paddington to Reading depot Night Riviera sleeper ECS. With the closure of Old Oak Common depot servicing of the sleeper stock is now done at Reading depot. 57603 was rebuilt from 47349 and introduced into service in December 2003.

47739 *Robin of Templecombe* passes Sonning cutting on 31 August 2010 with the 6Z47 Dollands Moor to Gloucester New Yard wagon move conveying new timber wagons, which had been imported via the Channel Tunnel. 47739 was named at Templecombe on 30 September 2008 by Colas driver Robin Gould and was dedicated to him as the last driver from the Somerset & Dorset Templecombe shed driving on the main line (started 1955). When 47739 was later sold to GBRF, the nameplates were transferred to 56049. (Simon Howard)

800001 passes Sonning cutting on 17 July 2016 working the 5X17 Reading to North Pole test run with 800002. (Simon Howard)

31601 *Devon Diesel Society* is seen west of Twyford on 7 December 2015 with the 5Z34 Bristol Barton Hill to Wembley LMD Empty Coaching Stock (ECS) move conveying a single refurbished mark three coach for use by Chiltern Trains.

60047 passes through Twyford station on 22 July 2017 with the 6V62 Tilbury Docks to Llanwern Steel Works empty steel train. 60047 was originally named *Robert Owen*, a philanthropist and mill owner who developed the New Lanark cotton mills.

66074 approaches Twyford station on 23 May 2015 with the 6L35 Didcot Yard to Dagenham Dock empty car train.

67005 *Queen's Messenger* pulls into Twyford station on 23 May 2015 with Statesman Rail's 'The Golden Arrow Statesman' charter train, which ran from Bristol Temple Meads to Canterbury West.

87002 *Royal Sovereign* passes down through Twyford station on 20 September 2018 while working the oZ12 Wembley to Didcot light engine move. The loco would then work the Didcot to London Paddington leg of the day one 'Out of the Ordinary' GB Railfreight charity charter train. This is believed to be the first time an AC electric has worked along the Great Western mainline under its own power. 87002, along with 86101 and 86401, is hired by GBRF from the AC Locomotive Group for use on empty Caledonian Sleeper stock moves between London Euston and Wembley InterCity Depot. (Simon Howard)

31601 passes Ruscombe on 12 October 2012 with a Bristol Barton Hill to Wembley LMD ECS move.

37516 passes Ruscombe on the Up fast line on 1 August 2011 with the 5Z94 Bristol Temple Meads to Southall ECS move.

Super power for the 7A09 Merehead Quarry to Acton Yard jumbo stone train as 59204 *Vale of Glamorgan* and 59001 *Yeoman Endeavour* pass Ruscombe on 1 August 2011.

59203 *Vale of Pickering* passes Ruscombe on 1 August 2011 with the 7C77 Acton Yard to Merehead Quarry empty stone train.

59204 passes Ruscombe on 12 October 2012 with the 7C77 Acton Yard to Merehead Quarry empty stone train.

60096 passes Ruscombe on 27 June 2015 with the 6V62 Tilbury Docks to Llanwern Steel Works empty steel train. 60096 was originally named *Ben Macdui*, which is the name of a Scottish mountain.

66707 *Sir Sam Fay – Great Central Railway* passes Ruscombe on 1 August 2011 with the 6V36 Bow to Appleford loaded spoil train.

67006 *Royal Sovereign* passes Ruscombe on 19 March 2016 leading the 1Z67 London Victoria to Bath Venice Simplon Orient Express.

High Speed Train set number 253 007 has the throttle wide open as it approaches Twyford with a Down service on 5 May 1981. The leading power car is 43014, which, in 2018, is in Network Rail yellow livery and used on the Network Rail Measurement Train. (John Dedman)

60071 *Ribblehead Viaduct* passes Waltham St Lawrence on 27 May 2012 with the 6V70 Lindsey Refinery to Colnbrook loaded aviation fuel train. The fuel is destined for Heathrow Airport. 60071 was originally named *Dorothy Garrod*, an archaeologist and the first woman professor at Cambridge University.

66001 passes Waltham St Lawrence on 22 July 2017 with the diverted 6M48 Southampton Eastern Docks to Halewood empty car train.

50033 *Glorious* in Network SouthEast livery is heading towards London at Waltham St Lawrence in May 1990 with a mix of matching liveried mark one and mark two coaches. Note how the nameplate has been repositioned so it now reads Glorious Network SouthEast. This loco was named in June 1978 after the battlecruiser HMS *Glorious*. (John Fox)

37893 in Railfreight Petroleum livery is heading 100-ton tanks at Waltham St Lawrence in May 1990. It is thought to be 6O8o, the 00:40 from Waterston Refinery to Langley Oil Terminal. (John Fox)

59201 passes Breadcroft Lane Bridge, west of Maidenhead, on 20 June 2014 with the 6M20 Whatley Quarry to St Pancras Churchyard Sidings Tarmac loaded stone train. 59201 was originally named *Vale of York*.

70010 passes Breadcroft Lane Bridge on 20 June 2014 with the 6M91 Theale to Earles Cement Works empty cement train.

59104 *Village of Great Elm* passes Breadcroft Lane Bridge on 20 June 2014 with the 7C77 Acton Yard to Merehead Quarry empty stone train.

66413 approaches Slough station on 23 July 2014 with the 6M91 Theale to Earles Cement Works empty cement train. Although seen here in Direct Rail Services (DRS) livery, 66413 was working for Freightliner. When DRS decided not to renew the lease on 66411 to 66420 they were taken over by Freightliner. 66413 lasted another four years in unbranded DRS livery, but was repainted into the new Freightliner colours of orange and black in 2018. (Simon Howard)

20142 sits in the bay platform at Slough on 18 May 2014. 20142 and 20189 were painted in Balfour Beatty livery and spent some time stabled here with two converted Freightliner Flats. The intention was for them to be used on the Crossrail OHLE Contract operating from the former Langley Oil Terminal sidings but sadly this work failed to materialise.

66601 *The Hope Valley* approaches Langley station on 3 July 2015 with the 6M91 Theale to Earles Cement Works empty cement train.

70017 is seen west of Tilehurst station on 16 August 2014 with the 4O27 Garston Freightliner Terminal to Southampton Maritime Container Terminal container train.

37607 and 37608 pass Purley Lane Bridge on 2 September 2011 with the 1Z59 Glasgow Central to Southampton Docks cruise saver boat train. 47841 was on the rear of the train to provide train heating.

Freshly repainted, 50044 *Exeter* passes Purley Lane Bridge on 2 September 2011 working the 0Z50 Cardiff Canton to Wembley Depot light engine move prior to working a rail tour the following day. Sadly whilst working a rail tour in July 2012 the loco suffered a power unit failure. The decision was made to purchase a power unit from a Portuguese 1800 Class loco, which are very similar to a Class 50 and with the same basic engine, and transplant it into the loco. After completion of the lengthy engine transplant this loco is now operational on Severn Valley Railway.

66105 passes Purley Lane Bridge on 2 September 2011 with the 4L36 Didcot Yard to Ripple Lane empty HTA coal hoppers. At this time there was a daily train moving stockpiled coal from a power station in London to Didcot power station, which itself stopped using coal in 2013 and is now solely fuelled by gas.

66147 passes Purley Lane Bridge on 2 September 2011 with the 6O26 Hinksey Yard to Eastleigh East Yard engineers train.

66417 passes Purley Lane Bridge on 2 September 2011 with the 4O49 Crewe Basford Hall Yard to Southampton Maritime Container Terminal container train.

70017 passes Westbury Lane Bridge on 13 July 2013 with the 4O27 Garston Freightliner Terminal to Southampton Maritime Container Terminal container train.

60010 passes Westbury Lane bridge on 31 March 2015 with the 6B33 Theale to Robeston Refinery empty oil train. 60010 was originally named *Pumlumon/Plynlimon*, which is the name of a Welsh mountain.

37607, 37409, 20305 and 47790 pass Westbury Lane Bridge working a single coach as the 5Z29 Crewe to Eastleigh on 28 March 2013.

66068 passes Westbury Lane Bridge on 2 September 2011 with the 6L35 Didcot Yard to Dagenham Dock empty car train.

66172 passes Westbury Lane Bridge on 2 September 2011 with the 6O15 Mossend to Eastleigh East Yard enterprise train. This train conveyed wagons for Fawley Refinery, Southampton Docks and Marchwood Military Port.

66193 passes Westbury Lane Bridge on 28 March 2013 with the 6X26 Hinksey Yard to Eastleigh East Yard engineers train, on this day running as an exception load due to the tilting point carrier wagons.

70018 passes Westbury Lane Bridge on 8 June 2013 with the 4O27 Garston Freightliner Terminal to Southampton Maritime Container Terminal container train.

Red kites are a constant companion when out photographing in the Thames Valley.

60099 approaches Pangbourne station on 28 May 2011 with the 6B33 Theale to Margam Yard empty oil train. In 2010 60099 was repainted into a Tata Steel silver livery and logo at Toton TMD and unveiled at Tata's Scunthorpe plant on 27 September 2010.

70013 passes through Pangbourne station on 18 July 2015 with the 4O27 Garston Freightliner Terminal to Southampton Maritime Container Terminal container train.

802006 is seen at Pangbourne on 6 August 2018 while working the 3C91 Bristol St Philips Marsh to London Paddington empty stock move. (Simon Howard)

31106 and 31465 double head the 6Z14 Eastleigh Works to Derby RTC test train through Lower Basildon on 13 April 2012.

31602, 57603 and 31601 pass Lower Basildon on 20 August 2012 working the 0Z32 Old Oak Common depot to Loughborough Brush Works light engine move.

37409 *Lord Hinton*, 37601 *Class 37-Fifty* and 47841 pass Lower Basildon on 27 April 2012 with the 5Z74 Eastleigh to Crewe empty stock working from the Cruise Saver boat train the previous day.

60091 *Barry Needham* passes Lower Basildon on 24 March 2017 with the 6B33 Theale to Robeston Refinery empty oil tanks. 60091 originally carried the name *An Teallach*, which is the name of a Scottish mountain.

66523 passes Lower Basildon on 24 March 2017 with the 6V27 Eastleigh East Yard to Hinksey Yard engineers train. On this occasion it included breakdown crane ADRC96713, which was returning to Bescot after assisting with a stone train derailment at East Somerset Junction.

68005 *Defiant* leads the 1Z16 Reading Triangle Sidings to Derby RTC test train past Lower Basildon on 17 July 2016. 68001 *Evolution* was on the rear of the train. (Simon Howard)

43185 *Great Western* leads the 1L58 Cheltenham Spa to London Paddington past Lower Basildon on 24 March 2017. 43185 was unveiled in 1988 Intercity Swallow livery at a fortieth anniversary event at the National Railway Museum in York on 2 October 2016.

31265 is heading a departmental working through the Thames Valley at Lower Basildon on 12 June 1978. The formation is mostly Grampus wagons loaded with dirty ballast with a brake van at either end. Behind the first brake van are two brake tenders. (John Dedman)

A very clean BR blue 47097 has charge of a loaded stone train made up of MSV tippler wagons near Lower Basildon on 12 June 1978. (John Dedman)

47185 is heading west at Lower Basildon with a short rake of flat wagons on 12 June 1978. (John Dedman)

47832 *Solway Princess* leads a Northern Belle charter train heading for Bath past Lower Basildon on 27 April 2012.

50049 *Defiance* is heading west with Mk1 coaches at Lower Basildon on 12 June 1978. 50049 was renumbered to 50149 and repainted into Railfreight livery in 1987 and finally withdrawn from service in 1991. It is now preserved by the Class 50 Alliance and is hired to GBRF for use on the main line. (John Dedman)

60163 *Tornado* passes Lower Basildon on 8 December 2012 with the Steam Dreams 'Cathedrals Express' charter train from Southend Central to Oxford. 60163 had joined the train at Acton Yard.

66061 hurries a rake of VGA vans along the Down main line at Lower Basildon working from Ludgershall to Didcot Yard on 27 April 2012.

33023 is heading east along the Thames Valley with a fully fitted rake of vacuum-braked four-wheeled vans with a brake van behind the loco on 12 June 1978. (John Dedman)

47090 *Vulcan* was one of the first Class 47s to be named when the Western Region named seventeen of their allocation at the end of 1973. On 12 June 1978 it was heading towards London near Lower Basildon in the Thames Valley with a loaded coal train with a good selection of wagons including 16- and 21-ton minerals and 21-ton hoppers. (John Dedman)

47790 *Galloway Princess* passes Lower Basildon on 8 July 2011 with a Cruise Saver boat train to Southampton Western Docks.

70001 *Powerhaul* passes Lower Basildon on 21 April 2012 with the 4O29 Crewe Basford Hall Yard to Southampton Maritime Container Terminal container train.

High Speed Train 253 033 is heading for London at Basildon with power car 43135 leading. A similar unit is heading west on 12 June 1978. (John Dedman)

70019 passes Lower Basildon on 21 April 2012 with the 4O27 Garston Freightliner Terminal to Southampton Maritime Container Terminal container train.

D1015 *Western Champion* is seen at Burghfield on 7 May 2016 working the 1Z52 'The Western Challenger' charter train from London Paddington to Okehampton. On this occasion D1015 was masquerading as D1010 *Western Campaigner*. (Simon Howard)

59005 *Kenneth J Painter* and 59002 *Alan J Day* double head the 7C77 Acton Yard to Merehead Quarry empty stone train past Burghfield on 26 April 2013. Kenneth J. Painter was a member of the Foster Yeoman team responsible for the introduction of the Class 59s.

43062 *John Armitt* is seen leading the New Measurement Train at Burghfield on 26 April 2013 working the 1Q19 Plymouth to London Paddington test train. John Armitt was chief executive of Railtrack, and then its successor, Network Rail, from 2001 to 2007. On 16 July 2007 Network Rail named New Measurement Train power car 43062 after him at London Euston.

60062 *Stainless Pioneer* passes Theale station on 13 July 2013 with the 6B33 Theale to Margam Yard empty oil train. The platform behind the train was built to allow passenger trains from the west to terminate at Theale during the rebuilding of Reading station. 60062 originally carried the name *Samuel Johnson*, an English poet.

60066 passes Theale station on 3 January 2014 with the 6B33 Theale to Robeston Refinery empty oil train. 60066 is in silver Drax Powering Tomorrow customer livery promoting the use of biomass as fuel for Drax power station. 60066 originally carried the name *John Logie Baird*, who is credited with inventing the television.

60092 waits for its booked departure time from Theale on 26 April 2013 while working the 6A69 Theale to Acton Yard empty sand train. 60062 originally carried the name *Reginald Munns*, a BR officer who worked on the development of the Merry Go Round (MGR) project for the delivery of coal to power stations.

Loadhaul livered 60007 approaches Theale station on 12 April 2008 with the 6B33 Theale to Margam Yard empty oil train. 60007 originally carried the name *Robert Adam*, the architect of King's Works from 1761 to 1769.

60074 *Teenage Spirit* is shunting at the Theale oil terminal on 24 January 2009 prior to working the 6B33 Theale to Margam Yard empty oil train. 60074 is in a special blue livery to promote the Teenage Cancer Trust charity. 60074 originally carried the name *Braeriach*, which is the name of a Scottish mountain.

60085 *MINI - Pride of Oxford* departs the sidings at Theale with the 6B33 Theale to Margam Yard empty oil train on 7 February 2009. On this day the train was diverted via the Berks and Hants route due to engineering works on its usual route. 60085 originally carried the name *Axe Edge*, which is an area of the Peak District.

60009 *Union of South Africa* passes Ufton Nervet on 23 July 2017 working a Steam Dreams 'Cathedrals Express' charter train from London Paddington to Weymouth.

57313 approaches Padworth crossing on 18 July 2015 working Statesman Rail's 'The English Riviera Statesman' from Ely to Paignton. 57316 was on the rear of the train. 57313 was rebuilt from 47371 and introduced into service in November 2004. From December 2008, locos 57313 to 57316 were hired by Arriva Trains Wales for use on a daily Holyhead to Cardiff diagram. After the Holyhead to Cardiff trains were taken over by Class 67s, these four Class 57s were sold to the West Coast Railway Company for use on charter trains.

59002 *Alan J Day* passes Padworth crossing on 26 April 2016 with the 7A09 Merehead Quarry to Acton Yard loaded stone train.

47854 *Diamond Jubilee* passes Padworth crossing on 18 August 2012 with NENTA Train Tours 'The South West Adventurer', which ran from Norwich to Plymouth. 57601 was on the rear of the train. This foot crossing was closed to the public once the electrification to Newbury was energised.

After being held in Towney loop, 60039 restarts the diverted 6B33 Theale to Margam Yard empty oil train on 17 January 2015. 60039 originally carried the name *Glastonbury Tor* and has since been named *Dove Holes* after the quarry in the Peak District.

70013 *Oliver Cromwell* passes Padworth crossing on 18 June 2011 while working 'The West Somerset Explorer' steam charter train to Minehead.

59204 and 66054 pass Padworth crossing on 13 July 2013 with the 7C77 Acton Yard to Westbury Yard empty stone train.

59004 *Paul A Hammond* approaches Padworth crossing on 24 October 2011 with the 7A09 Merehead Quarry to Acton Yard loaded stone train. 59004 was originally named *Yeoman Challenger* but was renamed *Paul A Hammond* at Cranmore on the East Somerset Railway on 21 June 1996 after one of the Foster Yeoman managing directors.

47832 passes Padworth crossing on 22 August 2015 with the Railway Touring Company's 'The West Somerset Steam Express', which ran from London Paddington to Minehead.

60054 approaches Aldermaston on 21 November 2015 with the diverted 6B33 Theale to Margam Yard empty oil train. 60054 retained Trainload triple grey livery with petroleum branding until overhaul in 2011 when it emerged in the DB red livery seen here. 60054 originally carried the name *Charles Babbage* who was a mathematician who built a calculating machine, a forerunner to the modern computer.

73961 *Alison* and 73964 *Jeanette* are approaching Aldermaston on 18 June 2016 with a GB Railfreight Staff Special from Ashford International to Weston-super-Mare. Commencing in 2013, ten GB Railfreight Class 73s were rebuilt as Class 73/9 by Brush Traction Wabtec at their factory in Loughborough. The main change was the fitting of MTU 1,600 hp V8 engines in place of the English Electric 600 hp engines, which makes them far more useful away for the third rail electrified network. Indeed 73/9s can now be seen throughout the UK rail network working test trains and in Scotland working sleeper services to Aberdeen and Fort William. 73961 was rebuilt from 73209 and 73965 was rebuilt from 73205.

6201 *Princess Elizabeth* passes Aldermaston station on 17 September 2016 with Steam Dreams 'Cathedrals Express' running from London Victoria to Plymouth.

70807 passes Woolhampton on 28 June 2015 with the 6C98 Oxford to Westbury Yard continuous welded rail train, which reversed at Reading. 70808 was on the rear of the train.

Wearing special commemorative livery, 43172 *Harry Patch – The last survivor of the trenches, the longest surviving soldier of the Great War* passes under Frouds Lane, Woolhampton, on 13 November 2016 with the 1A77 Exeter to London Paddington. This power car was named at Bristol Temple Meads on 6 November 2015 by Harry's grandson and last known surviving relative Roger Patch. Harry was a native of the West Country, born in Combe Down, near Bath, in 1898 and was the son of a stonemason. He was conscripted in October 1916 and eventually posted to the 7th Battalion, Duke of Cornwall's Light Infantry, serving as an assistant gunner in a Lewis gun section. On 22 September 1917, Harry was badly injured when a shell exploded overhead, killing three of his comrades. The inscription, taken from the poem 'For the Fallen' by Laurence Binyon, reads 'They shall not grow old, as we that are left grow old. Age shall not weary them, nor the years condemn. At the going down of the sun and in the morning, we will remember them.' (Simon Howard)

59101 *Village of Whatley* on the 7A09 Merehead Quarry to Acton Yard loaded stone train passes Midgham Lock on 20 December 2013.

59205 on the 7A09 Merehead Quarry to Acton Yard loaded stone train approaches Midgham Lock on 12 August 2013. 59205 has previously been named *Vale of Evesham* and *L Keith McNair*.

66509 passes Colthrop Crossing Box on 14 April 2012 with the 6A21 Cardiff Pengam to Theale loaded bogie hoppers. Colthrop Crossing Box remains open in 2019 to control three level crossings, the crossing adjacent to the box, the crossing at Thatcham station and the crossing at Midgham station. The footbridge from which this photograph was taken was demolished as part of the electrification of this line as far as Newbury.

60019 *Bittern* passes near the Newbury Nature Discovery Centre on 13 February 2010 with the Railway Touring Company's 'Valentines Express' charter train from Paddington to Bristol Temple Meads.

60103 *Flying Scotsman* passes near the Newbury Nature Discovery Centre on 21 May 2016 with Steam Dreams 'Cathedrals Express' charter train from London Paddington to Salisbury.

43012 approaches Newbury Racecourse station on 27 May 2016 with the 1C84 London Paddington to Penzance. This power car is in a special livery promoting Bristol 2015 European Green Capital.

45699 *Galatea* approaches Newbury Racecourse station on 13 August 2016 working the Railway Touring Company's 'The West Somerset Steam Express' charter train from London Paddington to Minehead.

59201 approaches Newbury Racecourse station on 27 May 2016 with a rake of empty stone hoppers from Acton Yard to the Mendip Quarries. As the pioneer Class 59/2, 59201 is fitted with a bell at one end, which can be seen here.

67008 enters the loop at Newbury Racecourse station on 24 October 2011 working the 3J41 Didcot Yard to Didcot Yard Rail Head Treatment Train. This train was usually worked by two Class 67s in top and tail fashion.

59004 *Paul A Hammond*, 60074 *Teenage Spirit* and 59203 *Vale of Pickering* approach Newbury Racecourse station on 11 October 2010 working the 7C77 Acton Yard to Merehead Quarry empty stone train.

50049 *Defiance* passes through Newbury Racecourse station on 12 February 2005 while working the 1Z27 Paddington to Westbury filming special. 50031 *Hood* was on the rear of the train.

37218 leads the 1Q19 Plymouth to London Paddington New Measurement Train substitute through Newbury Racecourse station on 20 December 2013.

Wearing Visit Plymouth promotional livery, 43163 passes Newbury Racecourse station with 1A83 Penzance to London Paddington on 23 August 2014.

67018 *Keith Heller* works the 1Z16 Bristol Temple Meads to London Victoria 'Venice Simplon Orient Express' private charter through Newbury Racecourse station on 21 December 2015. Keith Heller was the chief executive of English Welsh and Scottish Railway/DB Cargo UK.

66614 works the 6Y14 Westbury to Newbury auto-ballasters through Newbury Racecourse station on 27 May 2012. 66548 was on the rear of the train.

67023 stands in platform 3 at Newbury Racecourse station on 22 March 2017 while working the 1Z78 Tyseley to Bristol Temple Meads test train. 67027 was on the other end of the train.

Wearing HP promotional livery, 43148 tails a westbound service through Newbury Racecourse station on 15 June 2013.

66181 approaches Newbury Racecourse station on 15 April 2019 with the 6M20 Whatley to St Pancreas Churchyard Sidings stone train comprising of a rake of HRA wagons. Following the loss of coal traffic, 110 HTA coal hoppers have been cut down to around 80 per cent of their original length to create a fleet of HRA wagons for use on stone traffic. As stone is denser than coal, a shorter wagon is able to carry the same payload.

60076 passes through Newbury Racecourse station on 23 May 2015 working the 6V62 Tilbury Docks to Llanwern Steel Works empty steel train. 60076 originally carried the name *Suilven*, which is the name of a Scottish mountain.

70808 passes Newbury station on 5 November 2016 with the late running 6C26 Westbury Up Yard to Foxhall Junction engineers train. 70806 was on the rear of the train.

67026 stops at Newbury station on 23 February 2008 while working the 1Z31 London Paddington to Cardiff First Great Western rugby special. 67012 was on the rear of the train.

37248 *Lock Arkaig* pulls into Newbury station on 21 July 2007 with the Steam Dreams 'Cathedrals Express' charter train from Minehead to London Victoria. The return back to Minehead was worked by Bullied pacific 34067 *Tangmere*.

60063 passes Newbury station on 16 May 2015 with the diverted 6B33 Theale to Margam Yard empty oil train. 60063 originally carried the name *James Murray*, a philologist, lexicographer and editor of the New English Dictionary.

43002 *Sir Kenneth Grange* leads the 1A19 Bristol Temple Meads to London Paddington through the outskirts of Newbury on 27 May 2017, this service having been diverted via the Berks and Hants route during engineering work on the route via Swindon. Pioneer production power car 43002 was unveiled in original blue and grey InterCity 125 livery and named *Sir Kenneth Grange* by the man himself, designer of the iconic HST nosecone, at the public open day held at Bristol St Philips Marsh depot on 2 May 2016.

61306 *Mayflower* works engine and coach past Enbourne on the outskirts of Newbury on 27 November 2015 while working 5Z31 Bishops Lydeard to Southall.

66721 *Harry Beck* passes Enbourne on 28 August 2009 working the 4L31 Fairwater Yard to Whitemoor Yard scrap sleeper train. The sleepers, which form the load for this train, were recovered during operation of the track replacement train, which is based at Fairwater Yard in Taunton.

59101 *Village of Whatley* approaches the A34 Newbury bypass on 30 July 2012 while working the 7C76 Acton Yard to Whatley Quarry empty stone train.

59001 *Yeoman Endeavour* approaches Hamstead level crossing with the 6V18 Allington A.R.C. Sdg. to Whatley Quarry empty stone train on 25 May 2017.

59202 *Alan Meadows Taylor MD, Mendip Rail Limited* approaches Hamstead level crossing from the west with the 6L21 Whatley Quarry to Dagenham Dock A.R.C. loaded stone train on 25 May 2017. 59202 was originally named *Vale of White Horse*.

60019 *Port of Grimsby & Immingham* passes over the level crossing at Kintbury on 2 November 2012 with the 6M20 Whatley Quarry to St Pancras Churchyard Sidings Tarmac loaded stone train. 60019 has also carried the names *Wild Boar Fell*, which is the name of a mountain in the Pennines, and *PATHFINDER TOURS 30 Years of Rail Touring 1973-2003*.

The Great Britain IV was an epic steam rail tour that ran across the UK rail network over ten days. The final day's working, on 24 April 2011, was the 1Z68 Bristol Temple Meads to London Paddington, which was worked by 5029 *Nunny Castle*. It is seen here approaching Kintbury.

47760 approaches Kintbury on 24 April 2011 working the 0Z68 Bristol Temple Meads to Theale in support of 5029 on 1Z68 seen earlier. 47760 was attached to the rear of 1Z68 at Reading to later work the empty stock from London Paddington to Southall.

59104 *Village of Great Elm* approaches Kintbury on 3 August 2011 with the 7A09 Merehead Quarry to Acton Yard loaded stone train.

66207 approaches Kintbury on 3 August 2011 with the 6M20 Whatley Quarry to St Pancras Churchyard Sidings Tarmac loaded stone train.

59104 *Village of Great Elm* is seen west of Kintbury on 26 October 2018 with the 7C76 Acton Yard to Whatley Quarry empty stone train. Following the decimation of power station coal traffic, HTA coal hoppers can now be found working in stone trains from the Mendip and Peak District quarries.

59205 runs alongside the Kennet and Avon Canal at Kintbury on 26 October 2018 with the 7C77 Acton Yard to Merehead Quarry empty stone train.

59002 *Alan J Day* and 66152 *Derek Holmes Railway Operator* double head a rake of empty stone wagons at Hungerford Common on 15 March 2013.

59202 *Alan Meadows Taylor MD, Mendip Rail Limited* passes Hungerford Common on 21 September 2018 while working the 7C77 Acton Yard to Merehead Quarry empty stone train.

60076 passes Hungerford Common on 16 May 2015 with the diverted 6V62 Tilbury Docks to Llanwern Steel Works empty steel train.

59001 *Yeoman Endeavour* passes Hungerford Common on 7 September 2018 while working the 6L21 Whatley Quarry to Dagenham Dock A.R.C. loaded stone train.

37025 *Inverness TMD* passes Hungerford Common on 17 January 2019 working the 3Z23 Exeter Riverside yard to Ferme Park test train. 37025 is on hire to Colas Railfreight from the Scottish Thirty-Seven Group. (Simon Howard)

59203 passes Hungerford Common on 19 September 2018 while working the 6C31 Theale to Whatley Quarry empty stone train.

59204 passes Hungerford Common on 7 September 2018 while working the 7C76 Acton Yard to Whatley Quarry empty stone train.

59101 *Village of Whatley* passes Hungerford Common on 21 September 2018 while working the 6L21 Whatley Quarry to Dagenham Dock A.R.C. loaded stone train.

59203 and 59104 *Village of Great Elm* double head the 7C64 Acton Yard to Merehead Quarry empty stone train past Hungerford Common on 21 September 2018.

West Coast Railway Company's 37676 *Loch Rannoch* and 37685 *Loch Arkaig* storm through Hungerford station on 6 November 2011 with Spitfire Rail Tour's 'Sunday Positioning Growler' charter train from Exeter St Davids to Preston. 57601 was on the rear of the train to provide train heating.

60007 *The Spirit of Tom Kendell,* with its switch to safety branding, works the 6M20 Whatley Quarry to St Pancras Churchyard Sidings Tarmac loaded stone train through Hungerford station on 30 July 2012. 60007 was the first Class 60 to pass through the DB Class 60 overhaul program, being released into traffic in September 2011. Tom Kendell was a young engineer who sadly lost his life in an accident.

70017 is passing Southcote Junction on 29 September 2017 with the 4M58 Southampton Maritime Container Terminal to Garston Freightliner Terminal container train. Southcote Junction is where the line to Basingstoke diverges from the line to Newbury and the west of England.

70016 is approaching the foot crossing near Grazeley on 12 August 2013 with the 4M61 Southampton Maritime Container Terminal to Trafford Park container train.

66709 *Sorrento* is seen just north of Mortimer station on 23 May 2019 with the 6M26 Eastleigh East Yard to Mountsorrel empty ballast train.

70019 is approaching Mortimer station on 7 December 2015 with the 4O14 Birch Coppice Freightliner Terminal to Southampton Maritime Container Terminal container train.

47818 approaches Mortimer station from the north on 2 August 2011 while working the 1Z57 Edinburgh to Southampton Western Docks Cruise Saver boat train. 47790 was on the rear of the train. (Simon Howard)

60019 *Port of Grimsby & Immingham* approaches Mortimer station from the south on 10 January 2013 while working 6V38 Eastleigh East Yard to Didcot Yard conveying loaded tank wagons from the Fawley Refinery. (Simon Howard)

Hastings unit 1001 approaches Mortimer station working the 1Z92 'Andy Piper & Grant Tryon Memorial Train' charter train returning from Poole to Hastings on 7 August 2011. (Simon Howard)

57306 heads through Winnersh Triangle station on 18 June 2015 with the 1Z60 Manchester Victoria to Ascot 'Northern Belle' Pullman heading for Ladies Day at the Ascot Races. 57310 was out of sight on the rear of the train. 57306 was introduced into service in March 2003 having been built using parts from 47242, 47659 and 47814. (Simon Howard)

73951 *Malcolm Brinded* and 73952 *Janis Kong* are seen at Wokingham working 0Z73 Derby RTC to Ashford Up Sidings on 21 April 2019. 73951 was formerly 73104 and 73952 was formerly 73211. The two locomotives were completely rebuilt by Rail Vehicle Engineering Limited (RVEL) of Derby. Their 600 hp diesel engine is replaced by a pair of Cummins QSK19 750 hp diesel engines.

66055 is approaching Crowthorne station on 19 January 2019 with the diverted 6M48 Southampton Eastern Docks to Halewood empty car train. Due to engineering works between St Denys and Eastleigh this train was diverted via Fareham, Havant, Guildford and Wokingham before rejoining its usual route at Reading.

57314 leads the 'Northern Belle' into Bracknell on 20 June 2019 working 1Z50 Manchester Victoria to Ascot in connection with Ladies Day at the Ascot Races. 57316 was on the rear of the train. 57314 was rebuilt from 47372.

Black 5 44871 is seen shortly after departing Bracknell station on 23 May 2019 while working a London Victoria to Worcester charter train.

67012 enters Ascot station on 23 February 2019 with the 1Z69 London Victoria to Cardiff Central 'Venice Simplon Orient Express'. This train was run due to the Six Nations rugby match between England and Wales being held at the Principality Stadium. 67012 still carries the two-tone grey livery from its time working for Wrexham and Shropshire railways.